# Guard Your Body, Save Your Soul

POEMS

Laurie O'Brien

le chien noir press

This book is for all who work for healing,
especially Edward, Teresa, Martha, Anne, Marian,
Michael, Mary, Frank, Karen, Cynthia, Kathy, Thack,
Vicky, Joanne, Greg, Marion, Stan, Elmer,
Donna, Bill, Katie, Sarah, and Jack.

## Acknowledgments

*Apalachee Quarterly*:  Suppose Heaven
*Negative Capability:*  Light Has Always Attracted Them,
   *Ave Verum Corpus*
*Heaven Bone:*  Solving for *N*
*The Formalist:*  Apology
*Gulf Stream:*  Songs Bearing Weight
*River City:*  Cages for the Dead
*Cape Rock:*  Playing Bach
*Painted Hills Review:*  In Maine, *Dolce*
*Half Tones To Jubilee:*  Poem for the New Year,
   Cartography, Woman Dreams of Spaces
*Emerald Coast Review:*  Canticle for the Equinox,
   Here I Am, *Chiaroscuro*

Several of these poems first appeared in a chapbook
*Songs Bearing Weight* which won the 1994 Permafrost
Award and was published by the University of Alaska at
Fairbanks.

Support for the writing of many of these poems was
provided in the form of a sabbatical by the University of
West Florida.

# Contents

The title of this book comes from the Ministration
to the Sick from *The Book of Common Prayer.*

# I

---

# Time and Space

Terrible things are going to happen to people
you know. You are going to see the man
who coached your daughter last winter on the soccer field
lying in a hospital bed curled on his side
like a child while the hot wires of disease tighten
in his belly and the summer light lies across the room
like a shroud. Someone will tell your son what a jerk
he is because he is skinny and listens to the wrong
music and says dumb things in algebra class.
This is going to make him feel so bad that he doesn't
ask the girl with red hair to the eighth grade dance,
thus missing the chance to marry her and have her make
      him happy
for a lot of years to come. You are going to find out
that your mother had an affair with the baby doctor
when you were about seven or eight, and that all those
      times
when he came to the house on long sick afternoons
he was just hoping for a chance to step into the kitchen
and put his arms around the woman he wanted.
And then there will be the day when you hear
that your brother in his workshop has taken his wet
hand off a takeout paper cup of ice and Coca-Cola
and turned on the electric drill, shorting out all those
      circuits
of dreams he was carrying around. You are going to feel
pretty stupid for having loved the world as it is.

putting on your house like a borrowed jacket
lying down in a narrow bed and closing my eyes
trying to guess what the world will look like through the
          shuttered window in the morning

waking to my dog's first whimper
opening the door for him onto a green slope
ferns and cattails under the pines

all the way down to where the lake should be
mist against the far dark line of trees
summer sun at six already a blazing penny

coming through the last of the branches on its way up
a cat's cradle of birds hugging the tree trunks
darting from one succulent find to another

the red-headed woodpecker, cardinals, bee-sized
hummingbirds, all tiny blood drops of red on the green
          palette
Here I am changing the water in your vase of yellow
          sweet peas

feeding your dogs, throwing their sticks and balls
six clocks on the far wall from where I sit tell the wrong
          time
their pendulums swinging away in mild syncopation

Here I am where no one knows anything not the dogs or
        the birds
or the geese or the long striped snake we scared
        yesterday no one
thinks about endings or grief or anything left behind

# At the Edge ———————————————

*Martin Luther King Day, 1997*

All the roads out of my childhood seemed to lead past
    cotton fields.
The flat bottomland and the two-lanes edged with
    straight stands
of pine and hardwood—it was history, my way to keep
from going forward. I had the child's dislocation of time.
    What had been
might come back again, Rhett Butler, Roy Rogers, even
    Amelia Earhart.

The cotton was lush in its fields. I never saw anyone pick
    it, just the long
white rows going by in the car windows. It lay eager and
    soft in the bright sun,
like a bed or a grave. Downtown, my father's office was in
    the Cotton Exchange Building.
Front Street around the corner still held the names of the
    cotton brokers.
I loved this for a reason I couldn't name.

We don't ever know how we become a part of history. Is it
accident or design? My mother, puzzled in Memphis,
    thought it was
tacky to put out the garbage cans in front of the house
    when the alley
behind could better accommodate what was dirty,
    discarded, not wanted.
She could not hear the words that described a more
    dangerous thing.

Miles away I pretended to study for my last exam. The
　　　　assasination
caught up with me when FBI agents boarded our plane
　　　　on the runway.
My parents broke a citywide curfew to pick me up. On
　　　　the way home,
I saw tanks in front of the Plaza where we'd always gone
　　　　to the movies,
soldiers in Overton Park where we'd gone to make out
　　　　after dances and football games.

Everything is my history. This doesn't mean I understand
　　　　it or know it,
just that it's the continuum into which I've been born. I
　　　　was older
before I realized the Wild West and Southern belles had
　　　　ceased
to exist. *Correction*—they had never been. I cannot name
　　　　what drew me
to the Lorraine Motel each time I came home from
　　　　college.

I've numbered the little details of a life, kept them close,
　　　　understanding
that history names each one of us, moves us as counters in
　　　　a Parcheesi game
of time.  Sometimes it barrels us forward, sometimes it
　　　　creeps us back.
Nothing is ever a straight line, simple, elegant,
　　　　forgettable. The crooked

and strange are stamped upon  us, we are branded at
        birth with what is

off-center, with what lives at the colorful edges of the
        known world.
Nothing comes back, and yet everything does. Roy's
        riding Trigger in
a place I haven't gotten to yet. Amelia's in some other
        sky. We circle
the big events of the day, and then like the tides they
        reach out
and draw us in. We are chosen, then we choose.

Time is a geography. All of what was is a place,
flat as a table. Memory, like the old maps,
appears as that which we can fall away from.

The blue water of the mind is the feathered space
which sweeps against the ochres of countries.
We describe the surface, inking ourselves

into a magic circle. Here is the center.
It is always where we are. The angular coastline,
the dark hatchings of mountains, the curved fringe of
      rivers—

the gold leaf of borders is where we are going.
The fantastic edge, *terra incognita*, is what call us.

# Apology

As if we made it, we excuse the weather,
slant sheets of rain on crackling afternoons,
expected if not welcomed altogether.

We tell ourselves it loosens summer's tether,
the heavy pull of ringed August moons.
Reason enough for us to excuse the weather.

The lightning's metaphorical endeavor
to spark dry lives slipped badly out of tune
is just what we've been needing altogether,

although we're shy of making much of whether
the clouds are writing lessons in their runes.
Wait, it'll pass, we say, this weather.

The wind implies a stirring of the nether,
our green days sleeping since forgotten June.
Thunder rattles the doubts that draw us together.

The dialectic's easy to discover:
We watch the steady washing because soon
answers could be raining like the weather,
expected if not welcomed altogether.

*The original piece was written by Mozart in 1788. Edvard Grieg wrote the part for a second piano approximately 100 years later.*

At the distance of two pianos nestled in the curve
of each other, I cannot see your hands.
The sober space between us lies under
the pitch of the raised tops. We are the speaking
length of strings away. I can see
only the top of your head. Your nod says time.

I begin. *Primo*. One note spins out in time.
It is unfixed, briefly flies in an open curve.
This is an old piece, Sonata in C,
Sonata Facile, Mozart. My hands
have held these notes for thirty years, speak
now to the child, now to you under

the spell of the second voice running over and under.
This is a music Mozart never heard. Time
rushes back. Over the long years Grieg is speaking
to him, *secondo*. One singing embellishment curves
around the original score. On the keys our hands
are little rocking boats, the music is a sea.

The unknown beginner Mozart wrote for could see
perhaps the irony of the *allegro*. Under
her teacher's stern face her young hands
flew over the ivory keys while he kept time.
His gaze softened only when it fell on the curve
of her silk bodice, his music gently speaking

to her of intentions. Did he speak
about what lay beyond the music? Some urgency
might have led him to touch her hand and curve
her white fingers under
his own: in three days' time
his baby daughter Theresa would die in his hands.

Time bends the music under our hands.
A river of time walks through the pages before us
              speaking
of loss. Two voices parry, *andante, allegro,* and time
is still as strict and cold as constancy.
I am one pair of hands playing under
the spell of the music's long curve.

Only our hands know the urgency
of how the music speaks. We go back to the feel of the
              keys under
our fingers, to the relenting time, to notes bound always
              in the music's curve.

Think of the red-eared turtle as she lumbers
heavy with the lethargy of mud
from pond-bottom warmth into sharp
rank light of spring. It is a reluctant crawl,
this going out from where she slept, this
slipping out of safety into where
she knows she has to go. Some clock
has ticked her into leaving, has set
rough claws to drag her carapace abroad.
She is a blink and yawn into life, her lips
drawn back to taste the world again, cold
blood beginning to bubble along its way.
She is melody over a *cantus firmus*
of twigs and marsh grass, fugue of steps
moving with all the elegance of a man gone
blind but writing still the music that he hears.

## Woman Dreams of Spaces

At the edge of the day she peels back the onion dome
of the sky and her body, as if it had become
an ear, as if it were a shell holding
the whole ocean, hears stars rushing across
the black curve. The distances are great. Orion,
for example, must turn in his vast radius how many
times before he cartwheels down in the west?
The sound to her is as if skin has become
auricle, pinna, concha, canal, a window
into the polished labyrinth of heaven. Jupiter
and the Dog Star rattle their stored light. She dreams
of margins, boundaries, enclosures. Constellations learned
in childhood leave latticed lines on the air. The connective
tissue of space opens for her. She swims
in the perilymph, the watery landscape of imagined time.
Each space she dreams changes the boundaries of
            thought.
When the rooms are peopled, she moves there like her
            stars,
visible and untouched. Alone, she goes forward wanting
to travel the old illogical lines between lights.
The boundaries appear and dissolve, and she
is all blurred edges, becomes diffuse, cloudy.
Mornings, she trails the spaces behind her, surprised
by their little unseen fires which refuse to be
swallowed up in the common light of day.
What she understands is the way the doors open
upon each other, Chinese boxes her mind
strings out in sleep. They call her to follow.

Before the invention of letters, among the Egyptians,
the year was shown in the following way: they drew
a dragon that bit its tail, because they could see
how the year, even as it advances, turns back on itself.
Of its own accord it closes its mouth, coils in
to strike its own. *Ouroborous,* the Greeks called it,
leader, savior, guardian of a storehouse,
the tail-biting snake which shows the eternal
beginning again of everything, and also
the dangerous attraction of the self for the self.

Here is a morphology for us. The basic shape
of things is that some sacrifice is involved
in every redemption. The most useful symbol
contains its opposite. Here is the shed skin
of the snake, the small feather left
in the gaping nest, also the blood from the body.
Maybe it is all like rain, that which feeds us,
that which will bring something forth for us.

## II

# Binding and Loosing

The world will break your heart, living in it,
        going about every day.
I walk out, and the world happens to me, the
        light more than I can bear.

Each day I am less, each day I lose something.
        The cells flake off,
the body is diminished. There are tears for meat.

If I am in the desert, I understand it as a lovely
        place. What is there is watchful,
beautiful, wild, like the stone lion who sleeps with
        his eyes open.

The leaves blow away, the stillness in the air turns
        hard. It is possible
in the rattle of wind to hear an end to it all. At
        the intersection

of what is in the world and what we can see of it,
        we are born. The idea
comes in the telling, the clearness the stars say
        over again each night.

The hand reaches up. This is the sign of bounty,
        of what is given to us.
Also the sign of asking, of untying ourselves from
        all that we love and fear.

# Animal Husbandry

When everything is gone, how much remains.
Strip a room down to its bare walls
and it has the furniture of light. Peel off the surface.
Find the smooth sill where the long-haired cat
sleeps in the afternoon sun. Look at the face
of the dog who is steadily watching, waiting for dinner
or a walk. All these things of my life have their lives.
They will go on. My grandfather's cherry fourposter,
my mother's blue and yellow French crockery—it seems
they should have someone to tend them when I am gone.

Husband is to care for, to manage, finally to horde.
I have become the horder of all this,
the words in my books, the notes of my old piano,
the flowers planted at my door, the clutter that follows
my children. There is a holiness of space. It is filled
up with the acts and imaginings of good hours.

What does the one who husbands do at the end?
How to hand over what has been loved? This
is an old problem. No one has solved it. I know
I will have to give up what I have drawn tight around me.
I will have to leave behind all I have loved.

The first assignment he gave us was a self-portrait:
*a charcoal ground on a full sheet of drawing paper,*
*single light source, then draw with your kneaded eraser.*
As each stroke took away something
from chin, nose and forehead, the contours
of my face emerged. I hadn't known
eyes were centered on the front plane of the skull.
I was unfamiliar with the generosity of a mouth.
And how was I to deal with the problem of ears?

After that we drew what we couldn't see,
the contents of a paper bag, still lifes of apples
hidden in shadow. He dangled the lanky skeleton
from a hook and a line and made us draw
wrong-handed, never taking our pencils
from the page, never taking our eyes from the bones.
And the model, we drew her shyly,
carefully penciling in the bare flesh.

Draw from the inside he urged. No outlines,
no boundaries to separate the thing
from its world. Only the bright and the dark,
the mass and the emptiness which surrounds.

## Suppose Heaven

were punched out holes
in a paper sky and a cosmic
penlight pointed Orion, the little
Pleiades, familiar *W*
of Cassiopeia. Suppose something
we knew was tearing clouds
into strips and flinging them against
space where they clung and reflected
a small quarter moon. Suppose
someone drew the flat of a hand
over this water to still it before
slipping a body in, like you might
ease a new anemone into a waiting tank.

Tangent of light strikes
an arc of blue water, universe
of sky approaches infinity.
Pool's edge, there is the *s*
curve of a cat bending
to drink and a common factor
of birds, one song to a tree.
Below, the dog is reduced
to a quiver over a mouse
dying at her door. The equation
confounds, we multiply by jasmine,
divide by firethorn. If
the blus sky blinks, an answer
might be found. *N*
is the quantity of wonder in a backyard
acre, divisible only
by stars we cannot see,
predicting a simple going over,
the dead to the luminous.

# Cages for the Dead

Chickenwire and old wood warped
and bent is what they're made of;
one is the size of a baby's crib, the other
my length from head to foot. They stand
under tangled trees among old graves
where someone has been working. Brush
is piled in a dry pyre, new blankets
of white pebbles lie across the bodies
or where the bodies used to be—bones
now, or less, nothing animals
would be after, nothing to need
these fallen houses, shelter from the growl
and gnaw of hungry life. I could
reach down into the sandy dirt and touch
the baby daughters dying one spring
and the next, or the boy Curtis, nine, his *r*
inserted on the headstone as an afterthought.
It would not take much, I think, to cross
a boundary this thin, this dust and light,
this pale tangle of wild azalea vines.

# Light Has Always Attracted Them

Eleven hundred surplus army weather balloons
tied to an aluminum lawn chair
were what it took to levitate
the soul and body of Larry Walters
into the air above L.A. His cargo
was a six-pack, sack of peanut
butter and jelly sandwiches, CB,
and a bb gun he meant to use to shoot
balloons when he judged it was time
for him to be coming down. He planned
to hover above his own back yard, drift
over the neighborhood, see
the local sights from a different
vantage point.
          The world he knew
slipped by, toy cars and houses,
people, dogs, and trees, he left them all
like Legoland, forgotten. Currents
smooth as the flanks of his wife
bore all this ballast, wonderfully. He rode
the slipstream higher and higher into
light so clear he saw it wrap
its icy fingers around
the soft gray bellies of his balloons.

In bed, we imagine what we cannot see
running the rafters in the old house—
mice who are dancing us to dreams.
Listen, you say, they won't fall.
There's no need to watch,
just sleep.

First light pulls us out of sleep,
down to water's edge to see
how fish rise from the black to watch
our faces break the still roof of their house.
Leaves let go and one by one fall
down in the slow twirl of ending dreams.

Naked, you crash the cold where dreams
have settled in the iron muck to sleep.
Water takes you, in a flash you fall
over the silver surface and I  see
only the ripples and the house
with its thin chimney smoke, a watch.

For as long as you are under I watch
breathless while the chimney breathes its dreams
and the fish retreat. The house
waits you out, mice sleep,
and there is no moving thing for me to see
except the fading moon, her slow fall.

It is that fast, surprised time, fall.
Ink of maple and birch I watch
spread through the water, see
their colors over your belly and chest, dreams
wagging in your floating hair. You could sleep,
die even, under the unmoving water, in this still house.

Desire builds itself a house
beside a mountain lake in fall.
Under its roof lovers sleep
while the moon, fish, and mountain watch.
The chimney smoke bears up their dreams
for water and all the trees to see.

In the house now there is no one to watch.
If the mice fall into our dreams,
we will still sleep and no one will see.

# Canticle for the Equinox

This is the day the dead blink.
This is the day my daughter grows breasts.
This is the day the cows grow hungry and mourn the
        light.
This is the day dark clouds bloom out of the sunrise.
This is the day I hold the world outside the door with my
        breath.
This is the day when the pencil of light draws all things
        over again.
This is the day the memory of smoke returns.
This is the day the grass purples.
This is the day when cells of air talk to my body.
This is the day the taste of winter sits on the back of my
        neck.
This is the day for all that is ripe to wait, for the fields to
        lie still and dream.
This is the day husbands wake early and search for their
        younger selves.
This is the day the spaniel basks in her long coat as the
        cardinal sings to her.
This is the day the trees remember sleep.
This is the day the stars appear early, having traveled to a
        new corner of the sky.

The world holds
the sound of a ripe peach,
juice in a sweet surge
hiding
under the pressure
of a finger.

It is not sound
or thought, not memory
or desire,
only touch,
one finger
and then another
on the keys of the mind.

Consider that they may begin in the wood, in the shape
and bend and stretch of the curved and curled, in a place
where sounds fatten, then emerge.

Consider the thin filament of a bow raised in air
where first there is no sound, then the quivering breath
of strings under a touch.

Fingers on the neck search the raw. Hands
return over and over, probe the same ground,
search for what will come.

Tongue against reed tastes bitter juice, stroke
against membrane of kettle and tympani beats at the pure
soft flesh of a melody.

To play is to hang on the lip of desire where blood
sings *prestissimo*, where knees press the familiar warm
curve of the cello

and sound pours through the white air over the shoulders,
spreads like the burn of hands on thighs.

# III

## Crab

Crablike, the cancer sidled into my body.
I was busy with other things when it took over,
so I noticed only the pain. Gripped each day,
I accommodated it, moved slowly, apologized to all.

In a way, diagnosis is relief. I'm not crazy
or worse. I haven't imagined this new horror.
It's slipped in, taken over, planted its seed
in neglected soil and grown its profusion of starlike cells.

Name something and you own it. Like Adam
in his garden. I'm not ready to use the words.
If I call it something else, will it retreat?

Cancer, the crab, *karkinos* of the Greeks. Two
thousand years ago it appeared on Egyptian papyrus.
And we still don't fully understand.

God called the darkness of the first day night.
Could he have had Adam call cancer something else?
It's the old rose question. By any other name,
would it still threaten to kill?

In Samothrace, the statue of Nike stands headless,
        armless.
Once she was worshipped as the goddess of victory.
Now, like her, I am disarmed.

Disease tunnels into the body like fear.
It punches out holes in bones, plants itself
with the steadfastness of a stubborn weed.
Turn your back and it's taken root. Wait a few weeks
and it's over your head, grown six feet, a mile.

straight line of stitching where the breast used to be
                catheter dangling its foot of plastic hose
      bald head
        cooked skin
              folds where muscle had been
   yellow and missing nails
bare pubis

    me
    not me

but a body

    survivor?
        hard to say

no way to plan how long

        easiest not to look

## The Dreams of the Sick

With their eyes closed and consciousness set
down like luggage the sick ones slip into the other place.
Everyone is well there. Symptoms vanish.
There are no treatments, medications, surgeries,
visits to the doctor. There's no waiting
for test results, no need for special foods,
no compromise necessary with the body.

They get to this place with pills and prayers.
Once they realize its pleasure, they look forward
to going there. Under the hospital blanket,
at home between the soft sheets, they are all
alike, dozing and drifting, rising up like bubbles
so light are they without their various infirmities.
They are getting ready to leave.

Somewhere along the way the procedure changed from
        transplant to rescue.
The first was bad enough, the second admitted too easily
        the possibility of death.

But I get ahead of myself. The arcane vocabulary of
        disease begins to fall
away. For sixteen months I could tell you the exact value
        of my hematocrit,

the platelet count, the magic number of white cells. At
        one point I learned
the stages of mucositis, the progression of dehydration,
        and even the way

a Demerol IV push was halved, the seconds that had to be
        counted
before the rest was given. *Normal* they say now, and I
        don't even ask.

No details beyond what can't be ignored, the bruises, the
        spine shorter by an inch or more,
the ungrowable hair. It could be a miracle but I've never
        been one for too much optimism.

Over beers at the neighborhood deli we discuss the
        importance
of denial, how good it is to work, go shopping, gossip,
        pretend

we are just like everyone else. Clothes, cats and dogs,
        children, it turns out, absorb us
more now than painkillers, range of motion, the
        persistent inscrutability of our doctors.

Some days I just don't feel rescued. The lifesaver hurled in
        my direction floats
at the end of its tether, and I can't tell yet if I'll be able to
        reach it or not.

I am in such a space that I say over and over
*one year ago today.* The ordinary becomes an anniversary.
I've always done this. My brother taught me. *Think
back,* he said, *to what you were doing each Fourth of July.*
He could go back decades. Younger,
I could only reach a few past years.

Now I reckon a single year, a year whose days
I have marked and counted, perhaps as a way
to have them if I am not to have anything else. Fall
was the season of finding out, winter the season of
          hospitals.
Snow at the window and the talk of snow going on
          around me.
Christmas Eve peppermints on my bedside table
from the Cancer Society lady. New Year's
the best nurse off duty so she could party.

My brother remembered the fireworks, a little
different each year. Remembered the sunsets
and who brought the picnic. Remembered
even without having anyone to tell.

Who can I tell of the fear that gripped me
one year ago? Brought by a friend to the hospital
hours before daylight I was almost certain
I couldn't go in. Once inside, I couldn't talk.
Once in my hospital bed, I couldn't think.

One year ago I remember confusion about the surgery—
radical, modified radical, what did it matter? I wanted it
        over,
only wanted to sleep, to dream the dreams of the well,
to remember when I was safe, when my body was whole.

The body heals. One year later I can see
in the bathroom mirror that the skin is all of a color.
The long red line of the scar has soothed itself
into a pale crease. The gathers where skin
was stitched, layer upon layer, have subsided.
The chest is smooth, unfinished looking. There
is a pattern of depressions, hollows,
where the lymph nodes had been.

Someone asks me about chest wall and muscle.
How do I tell? The scar jumps when the muscle is
          tightened.

What is most startling still is what is missing.
It is not hand or eye, kidney or foot,
but there has been a severing, an amputation.
Where there was flesh, blood, milk is only air.

When my daughters were babies I always put them first
each morning to the left breast. Now it's gone.
What can I say about what I can never have?

## About Her Death

I tried to warn you that it could happen,
that any one of us could go from lunch and chit chat
to the morphine pump pretty quickly.

Only a few weeks. Of course she didn't tell us
how she hurt. And me? She had asked
questions. I missed the danger behind them.

*Brain, lesion, return* hung in the hospital air.
The body under the white sheets shrank
to that of a child. The red polish on her toes

wore away. The family tried to keep us from coming.
She doesn't recognize anyone, they said,
but she did. She knew us all.

It had rained for a week when we buried her.
Summer thunder ruffled the funeral tent. The men
held their umbrellas high, the women in black

stepped gingerly on sodden earth. The crowd
was large. I wanted to ask *how well did you know her?*
*Had you seen her scars and her burns?*

Only a week after her death I realize
the space she has left, the places I picture
her where she can never be.

# Father Larry Asks for a Poem

He's older but not old and wears a body no one would
        want.
His neck is a raw stripe from radiation, his thin chest
in its cleric shirt a repository for cells run amok. The
        voice
is a rasp, a loose rattle. My children recognize it now
instantaneously when he calls.

He lives alone. He drives his bright red car each morning
to the church, methodically conducts his meager business.
He tells me Friday last he started coughing blood. I'm
        back,
suddenly, in an English class from long ago. *Think
        about it,
says the professor, the poet Keats who'd nursed his brother
until death sees in his own handkerchief the first red streaks
and knows how his own life will end.*

We joke about the odds. I tell him he must not
live out the doctor's prophecy of numbers, some
years, some months. But he's planned his funeral,
even bought the candle that will burn beside his body in
        the chapel.

Each day it seems there's more of an accumulation before
        death—
his cane, a back brace, pills, peculiar foods. It is the
        progression
we all dread, the calling back of the body to its dust. I put
my hands upon him, and his skin is feather light, almost
        not there.

# Not Walking Around

I imagine how it will be,
the single step
down to my living room putting
the good sofa, the fireplace, my piano
out of bounds.

I imagine not
being able to step up
into my Jeep, not
being able to navigate
the long path through the woods
to my building or the steps
upstairs to my office.

I imagine how small
the universe will grow,
telescoping down
to the pair of windows
across from  my bed,
the light shaken
through the pittosporum leaves.

To let go of the world is hard.
Place, shadow, scent, and breeze—
I have loved them all.

The body when it is trying to leave speaks loudly.
Each flutter of the eyelid, each pursing of lips
is a cry saying if it were only up to me I would stay here.
The hands rest on the white hospital sheets.
They are mostly still. The hair is shorn, the skin is like
     wax.
The scars are familiar, a part of this dying,

Death rattles the heart, it is a hot wind which cannot find
     its way.
The final catastrophe is what is essential to all of us.
Grief shows how we love the body even when it is sour
and breaking and wanting to get away. Language
and memory, the chimerical soup of our hearts,
brings us to the irreducible edge, here, at the bed of
     death.

The body is a boundary, a membrane always about to
     break,
always ready to slip past the living into the great space of
     the dead.
We call out to it, we lay our hands on it and try to hold it,
but we are too late. The quick and the dead, we say to
     ourselves,
but we have got it wrong. The dying are eager,
they are ready to go, they never look back.

# IV

## How To Bind a Dog

What I tell myself is that all the testosterone I need
is contained in the body of one seventy-five pound black
    puppy
whose usual greeting is a nose to the crotch.

I say he's my boy, my man, my good dog,
sweet boy, Black Jack, big-footed bringer of treasures.

Already I know his desires, how he launches
himself from my arms into blue water, his webbed feet
    barely
parting the surface, his breathing heavy and intent.

Like all lovers, he's a thief: cat food, a little
redolent garbage, the new Nine West pumps.

When I bury my head in his fur, I smell safety,
the warm puppy odor of adoration, exalted essence of
    need.

I forgive him his transgressions, the gnawed leg
of the coffee table, stain on the dining room carpet.
I understand excess. It is what comes when love is new,
    before there are limits,
when exuberance is the main course.

At night I lie down, and the comfortable bulk of him
stretches beside me. He's a good dog, even in sleep,
his small burps and hiccups of peacefulness announce his
    dreams.

## Tender

Is it possible he knows that what he does
can be interpreted? Or does his dog's life
preclude examination, interior or otherwise?
This is the ritual: he ranges around the bedroom
with his chew toy until I turn off the reading light.
I call him and he jumps up, then settles halfway down
my grandfather's bed. He's a top-of-the-covers
dog, a snuggler, but only  when it's cold.
He sleeps facing away, his long body stretched
so that rump and tail are within reach, head
and forepaws are tucked in the curve of the footboard.
Settled, he sighs. It's deep and thorough, what
we used to call in childbirth class the cleansing breath.
And then he lays his head over my feet. I could say
protective but he's not, especially, having never had
any real reason to be. So maybe it's his comfort,
or even random behavior. But I'll take tender,
reciprocation for dog food, toys, good walks.
Maybe tender isn't planned, just is.

In the deep December night
the soft rumble of his voice
climbs a scale of ascending dreams,
proffers a reassuring noise.

Beside me in the bed he lies,
sentinel flesh, easy to rouse,
but lost, lost now in his rabbit world,
leaving the stars to keep this house.

The press of fur, the heft and weight
of body beside me as I sleep
proves even oblivion casts
a wide net which keeps us safe.

## How to Bind a Dog

Take your short braided leather lead
in your left hand and double
it over until there is just a straight line
between you and your dog.
Have him sit at heel. Get
his attention. You can do this with
a command *watch* or even
with a small piece of food held
between your front teeth. Sitting
straight on his haunches, he should look
at you with his head slightly cocked,
chin up, eyes eager. You keep
your shoulders squared. Your look
will be sideways, conspiratorial.
Say his name. His ears will prick up.
Step smartly forward on your left foot,
left hand with lead firmly planted
on your hip. Practice a lot. Know
that all by himself he'll begin to add
an initial bounding  for joy.

In the dog class we practice
training the invisible dog.
Dead serious, we heel briskly
around the ring. The trainer
shows us the turns, the fourth position
ballet step of the right, the tight *t* of the left.
*Watch* we say to the dog who
isn't there, engaging
his imaginary attention.
In the space beside us we see
the friendly head lifted,
paws and tail held high.

Around the green rubber mats we move—
forward, halt, about turn. *Hustle*
we whisper to the invisible laggard.
Our steps are small, controlled, but quick.

The goal is to move lightly
like Baryshnikov who dances barefoot,
having given his shoes away.

## Dog Toys

The world is divided
into what's his and what's mine.
I can see the demarcation clearly,
but for him it's all of a piece:
sofa cushions, bathing suits, underwear,
all shoes. I'm willing to concede
the gray zone, towels left by the pool,
plastic cups, occasional garbage.
But having lost three garden hoses,
the window screens, four patio chairs,
I'm working to contain the damage. So far
he's taken kindly to the rubber porcupine
and floating Kong, knucklebones, all squeaky balls,
and hamburgers—rubber or real. He likes
a strong rope to wage war on. He'll take
a rawhide bone just before sleep. But none
of this keeps everything else safe. Whatever
treasure is piled up in his kennel or by
the back door, he's always looking for more.
His toys, it seems, fill a space in his life
but never enough of it. He must think that
by gnawing my good sneaker he
can chew his way straight into my heart.

No pedigree, my daughter declared right from the start.
She only wanted a dog whose life she could save.
She who cannot save her own, and cannot save mine.

So this is how we come to be mothers, both of us,
to a week-old dog, a pound and a half of fawn fur
with a black hungry muzzle, eyes just opened, still unable
        to walk.

In the supermarket we buy a six-ounce baby bottle, two
        nipples,
a can of evaporated milk, yogurt. It's been fifteen years,
I calculate, since I last visited the baby aisle.

The routine of feedings comes back in a rush. The strong
        suck
of the little mouth gratifies. She sleeps in fullness, in the
        easy
equation of warmth and safety. We have done this for her.

Over and over we tell the stroy. Someone abandoned the
        litter
in the box compactor behind the old Winn Dixie out in
        the country.
The vet next door heard them crying when he came to
        work.

Who could do such a thing, everyone asks? Eight of them
slowly starving. It's too much misery, too close to think
about what keeps us safe, comforted, full.

Long-legged, rangy, the puppy is growing rapidly
from the desperate week-old being who had to be coaxed
to suck. We watch her now, full of herself,
climbing on Jack the big lab, nipping his ankles
and muzzle, pushing her nose up under his wagging
tail. He's a frontier, a continent for her to explore,
she who has never known mother dog. She has
only had us, so he must be at once
exotic and familiar. I imagine her thinking
*I must be one of these* as she slides over
his resting haunches, rolls on her back between
his long forepaws. His tongue is a damp blessing.
Even with her head in his jaws she has nothing to fear.

On the last day of the year I take my dog
north to what passes for woods around here, tall pines
and scrub. When we're a few miles away from our turn,
when the strip malls give way to the fire ranger's station
       and finally
to cotton, he understands—vocalizes, as they
say of dogs—his eminent and remembered pleasure.

At the lake he is visited by geese, nine
gray-flecked with white bottoms and orange bills,
two white, like swans. Their flotilla steams over to where
he swims at the end of the dock. They are curious
about the splash of dog and ball, unruffled
by the presence of what might be predator.

       But he isn't.
He's confined in the loop of water and sky,
master and blue rubber ball. Who's to say
his system is simple, that what has evolved for him
is any less valid than the vestments and symbols we
put on in our need to touch what is holy?

It turns out that what is blessed is often unnoticed,
messy, disruptive, the wet dog rolling in red clay,
sand, and pine straw. And what is given to us
seems at first like nothing we ever wanted.